W9-AHS-942

8/12

Eisenhower Public Library
4613 N. Oketo Avenue
Harwood Heights, IL 60706
708-867-7828

FIRST GRAPHICS

Triceratops:
THREE-HORNED GIANT

by Mari Bolte   illustrated by Jason Dove

CONSULTANT:
MATHEW J. WEDEL, PhD
PALEONTOLOGIST AND ASSISTANT PROFESSOR
WESTERN UNIVERSITY OF HEALTH SCIENCES, POMONA, CALIFORNIA

CAPSTONE PRESS
a capstone imprint

First Graphics are published by Capstone Press,
1710 Roe Crest Drive, North Mankato, Minnesota 56003.
www.capstonepub.com

Copyright © 2012 by Capstone Press, a Capstone imprint.
All rights reserved.
No part of this publication may be reproduced in whole or in part, or
stored in a retrieval system, or transmitted in any form or by any means,
electronic, mechanical, photocopying, recording, or otherwise, without
written permission of the publisher.
For information regarding permission, write to Capstone Press,
1710 Roe Crest Drive, North Mankato, Minnesota 56003.

 Books published by Capstone Press are manufactured with paper
containing at least 10 percent post-consumer waste.

Library of Congress Cataloging-in-Publication Data
Bolte, Mari.
  Triceratops : three-horned giant / by Mari Bolte.
    p. cm. — (First graphics. Dinosaurs)
  Includes bibliographical references and index.
  Summary: "In graphic novel format, text and illustrations present Triceratops, its
characteristics and probable behavior, and information about extinction"—Provided
by publisher.
  ISBN 978-1-4296-7601-4 (library binding)
  ISBN 978-1-4296-7931-2 (paperback)
  1. Triceratops—Juvenile literature. I. Dove, Jason. II. Title.

QE862.O65B65 2012
567.915'8—dc23   2011036563

EDITOR: *LORI SHORES*
DESIGNER: *LORI BYE*
ART DIRECTOR: *NATHAN GASSMAN*
PRODUCTION SPECIALIST: *KATHY MCCOLLEY*

Photo credit
Shutterstock:sgame, 6 (tank)

Printed in the United States of America in Stevens Point, Wisconsin.
102011   006404WZS12

TABLE OF CONTENTS

THE AMAZING TRICERATOPS

The ground shakes. Branches break.
Large animals stomp toward the river.

AGE OF THE DINOSAURS

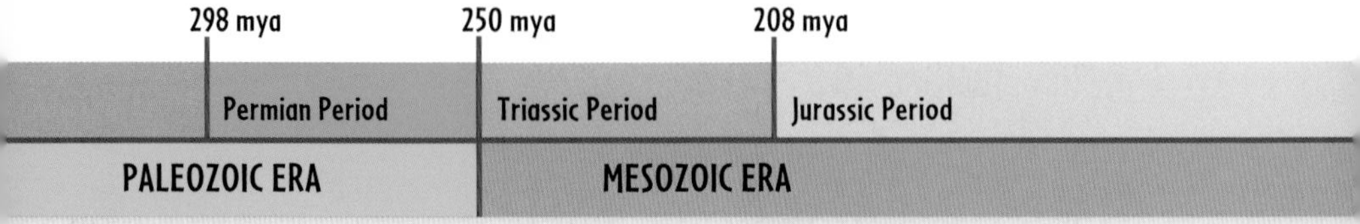

	298 mya		250 mya		208 mya	
		Permian Period		Triassic Period		Jurassic Period
	PALEOZOIC ERA			MESOZOIC ERA		

It's a herd of triceratops. Their name means "three-horned face."

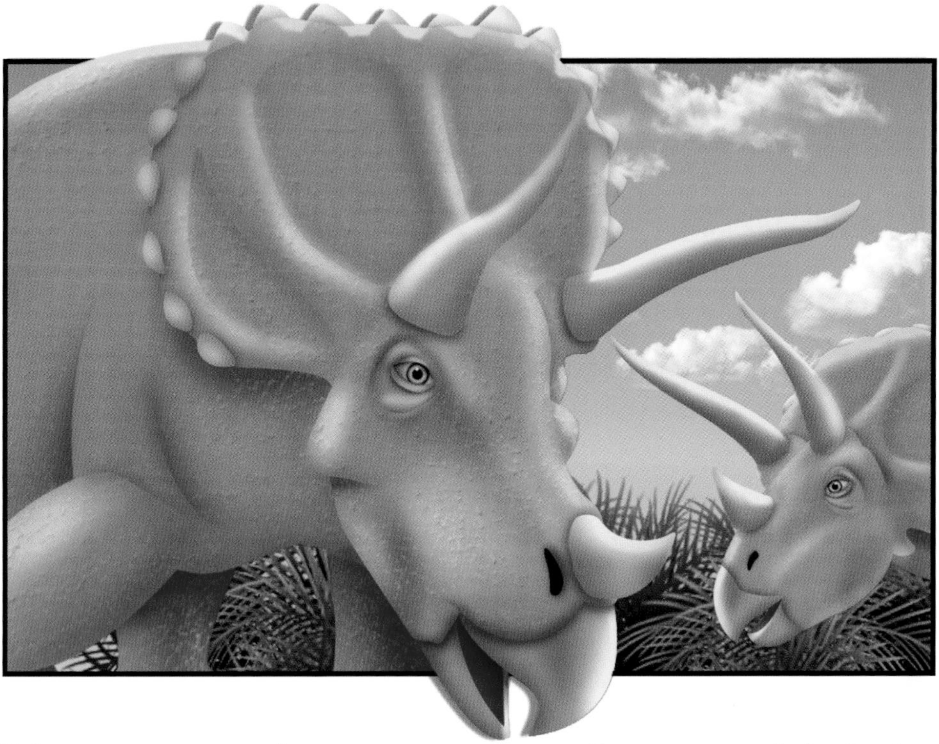

Triceratops are the most common dinosaurs of their time.

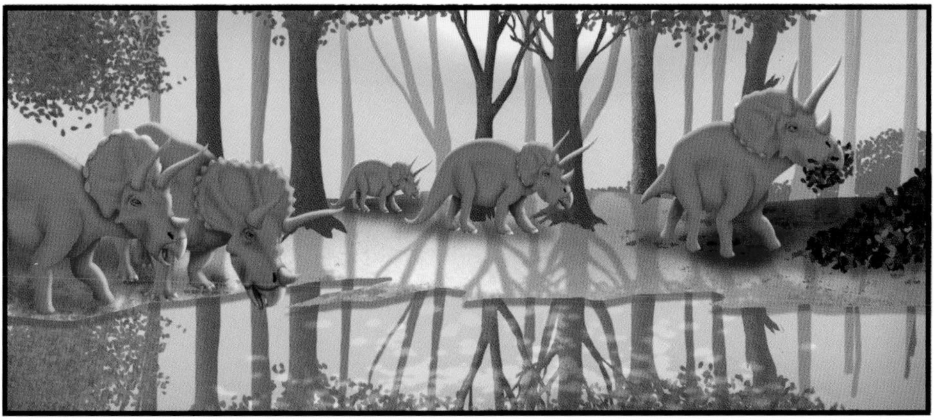

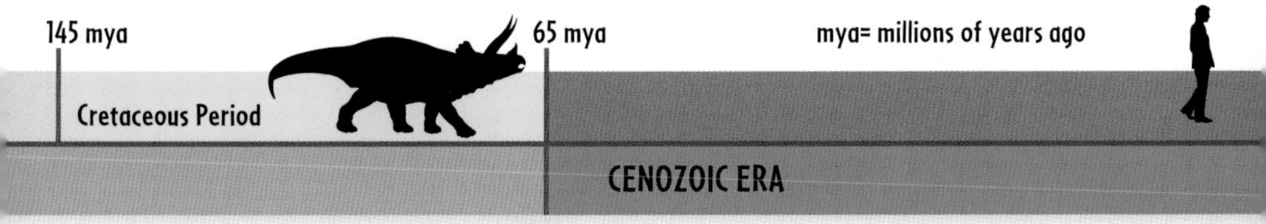
145 mya
65 mya
mya= millions of years ago
Cretaceous Period
CENOZOIC ERA

An adult triceratops was almost as long as a tank.

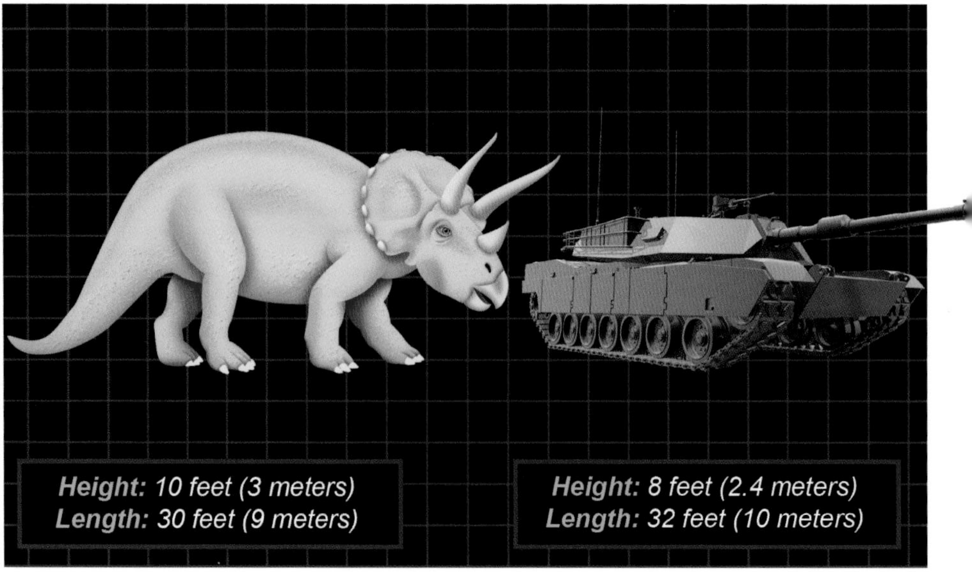
Height: 10 feet (3 meters)
Length: 30 feet (9 meters)
Height: 8 feet (2.4 meters)
Length: 32 feet (10 meters)

Triceratops' frill was 7 feet (2.1 m) wide.

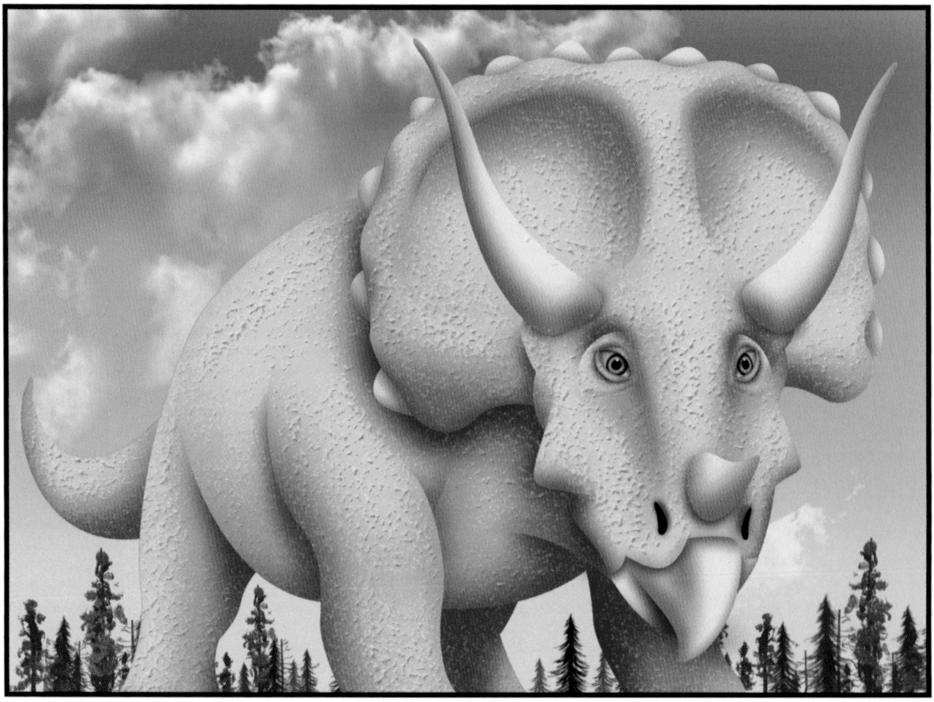

The frill made triceratops look bigger with its head down.

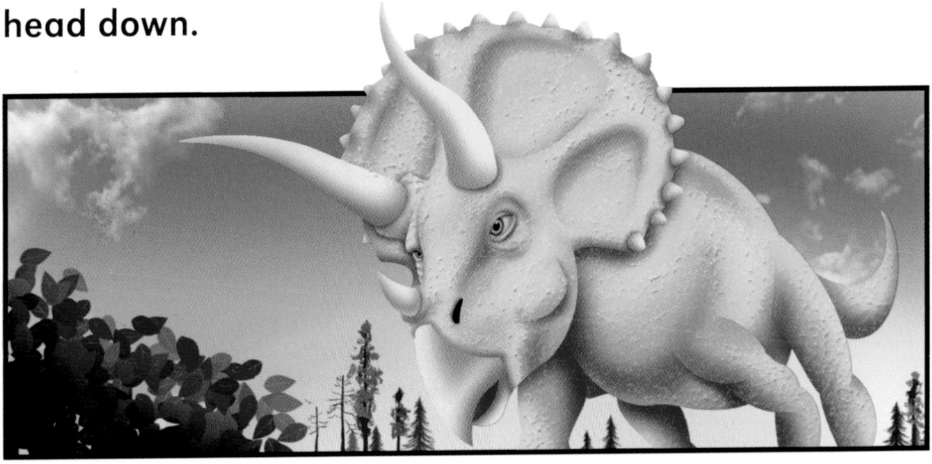

The bony frill also protected triceratops' neck.

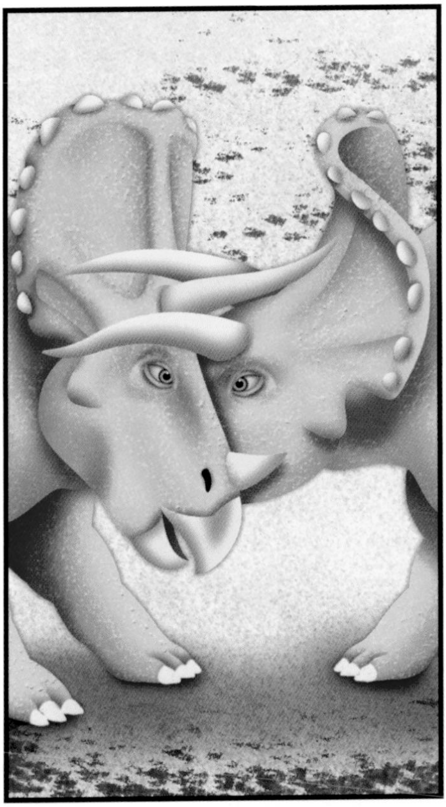

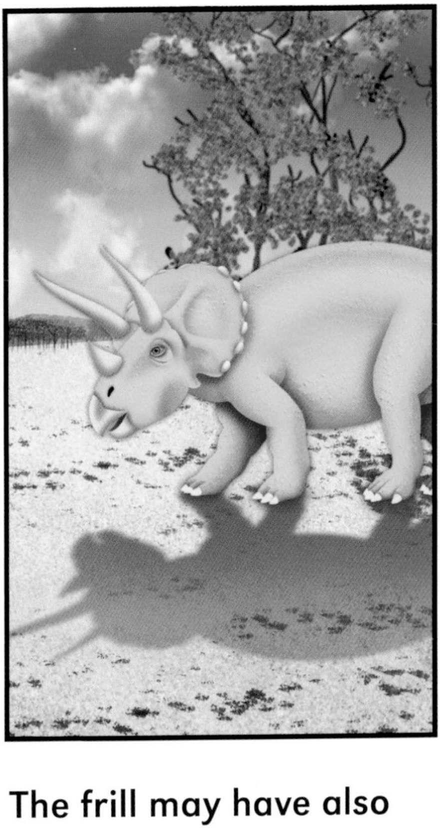

The frill may have also helped triceratops stay warm or cool.

Torosaurus looked much like triceratops.
It had a frill too.

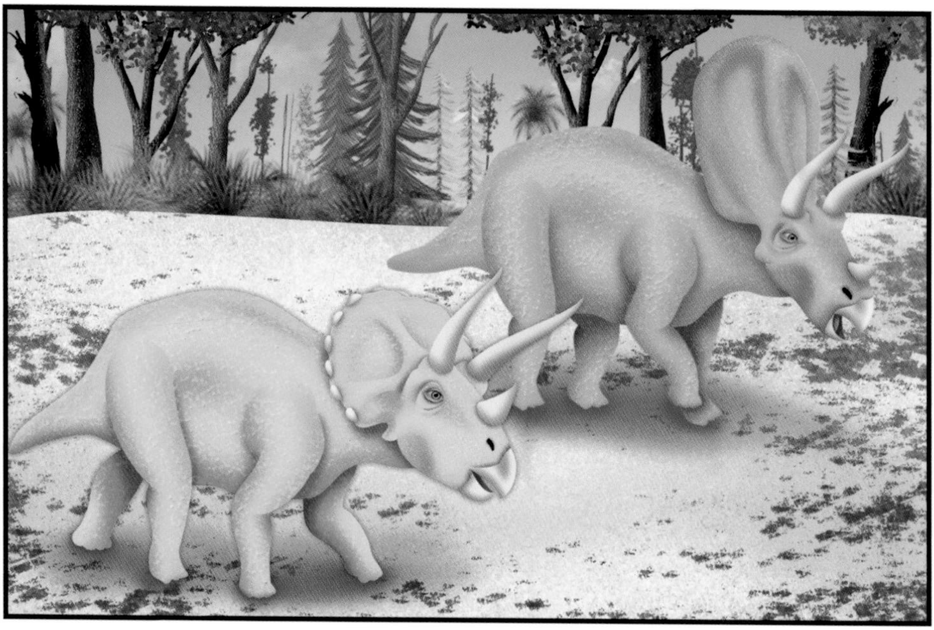

But torosaurus' frill was larger.

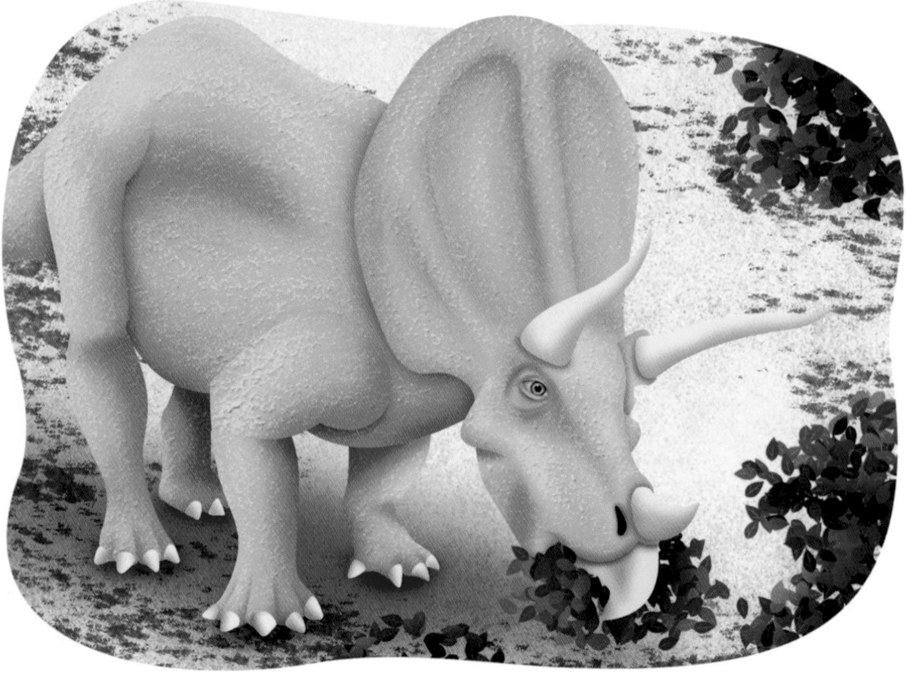

Its frill also had two large holes covered by skin.

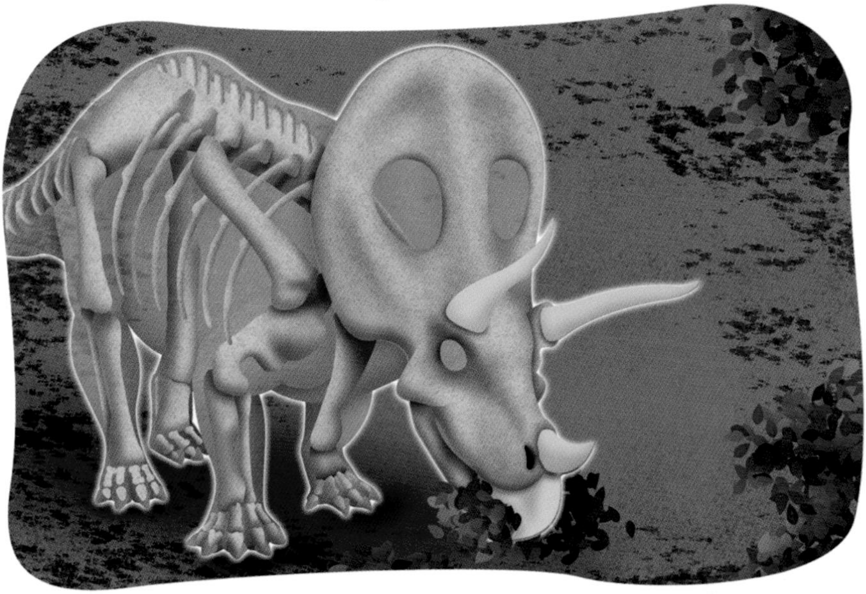

Some scientists think torosaurus was an old triceratops. The frill may have gotten larger as the dinosaur grew.

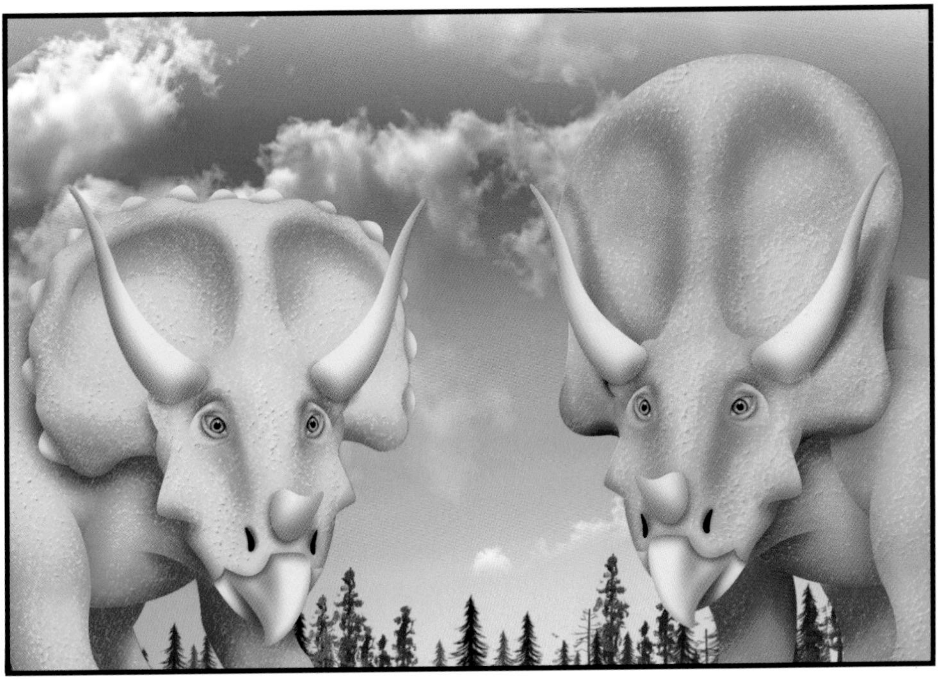

WHAT'S FOR LUNCH?

Many plants grew in North America where triceratops lived.

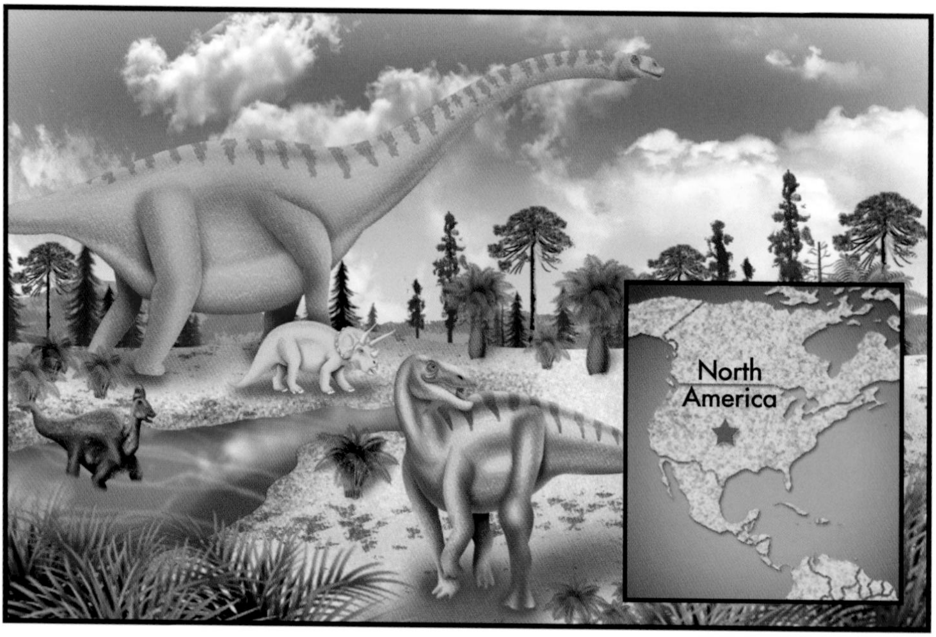
North
America

Triceratops ate plants. Its strong beak easily bit through buds and leaves.

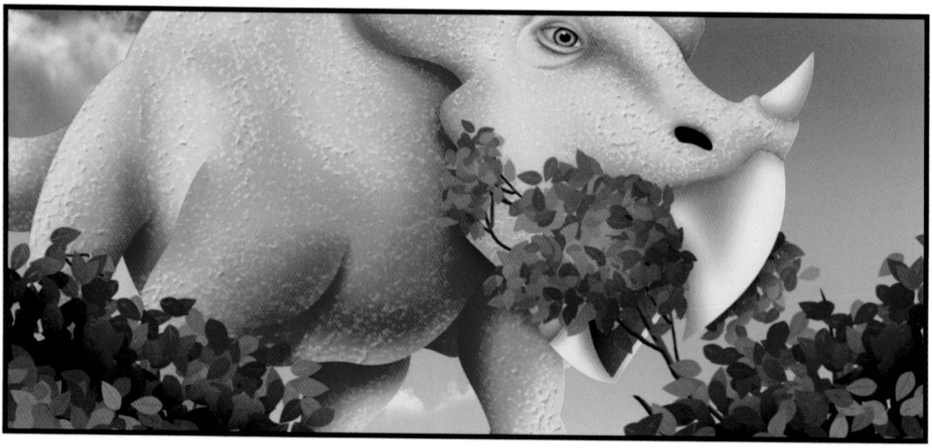

Sharp teeth rubbed together to crush tough plants and stems.

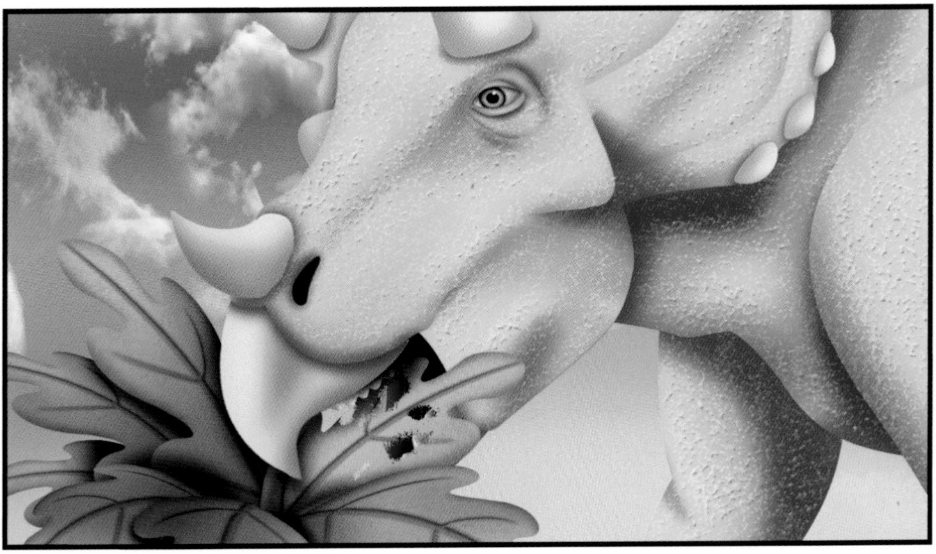

Triceratops had rows of closely-packed teeth. When old teeth wore down, sharp new teeth moved forward.

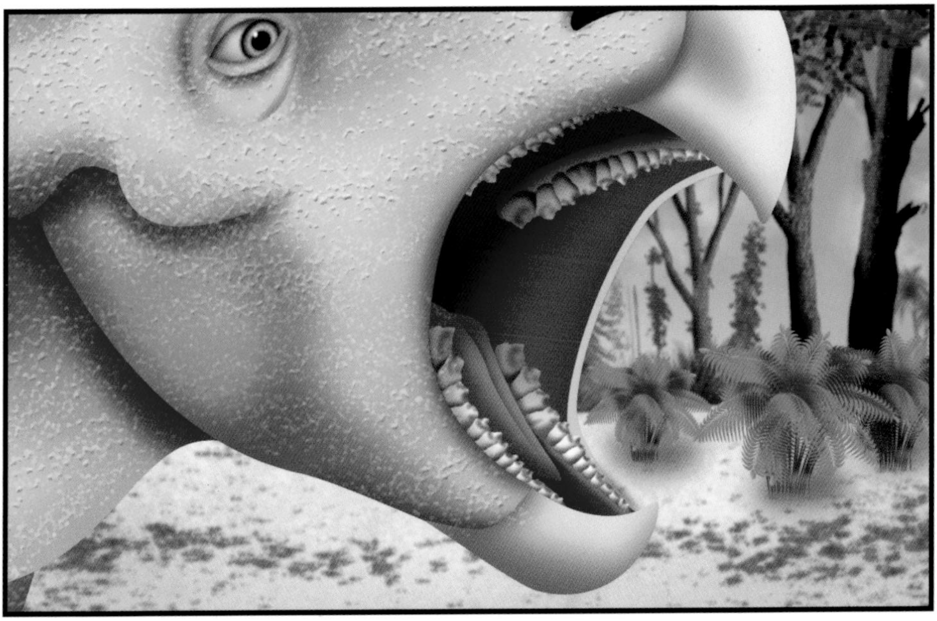

TRICERATOPS TOGETHER

Baby triceratops hatched from eggs.

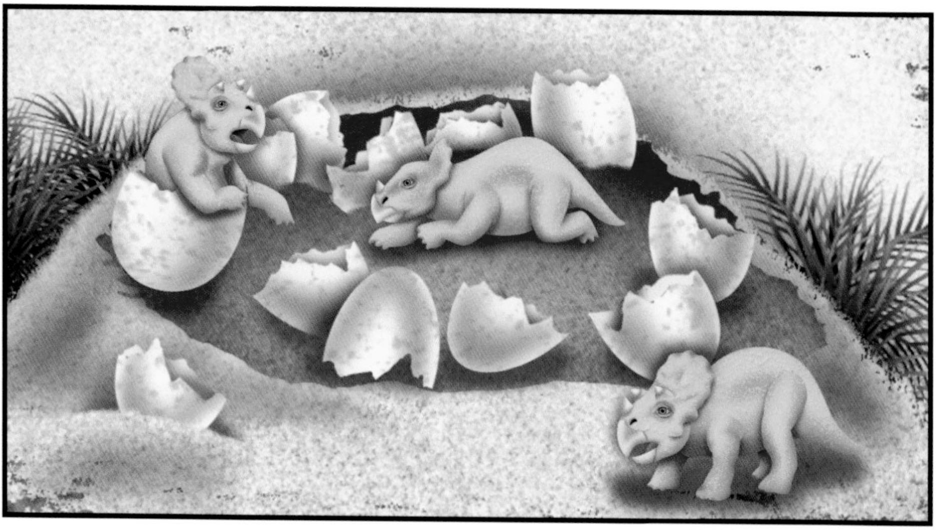

POW! Young triceratops practiced using their horns.

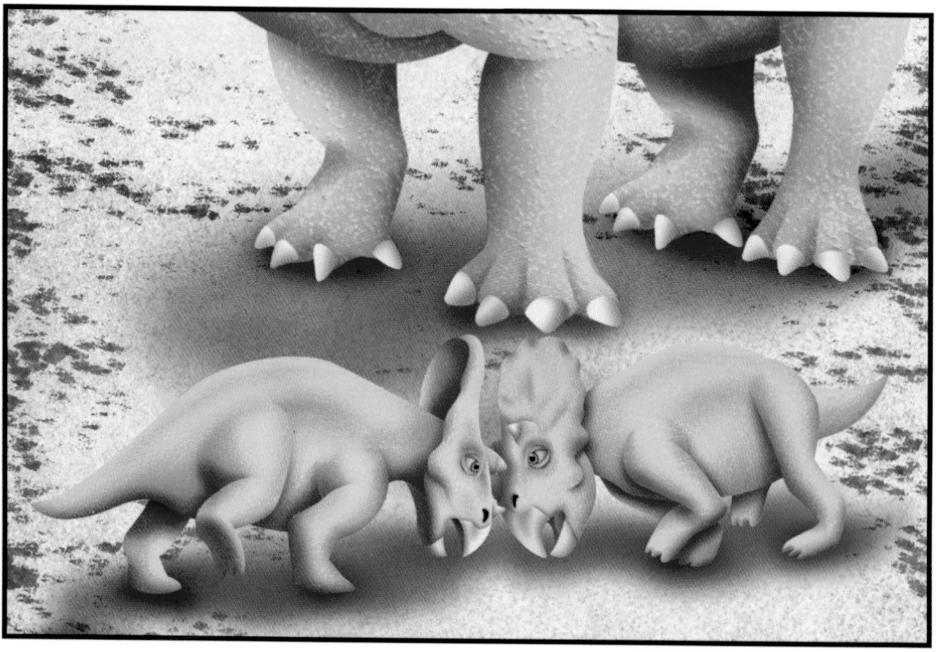

Triceratops lived in large herds.

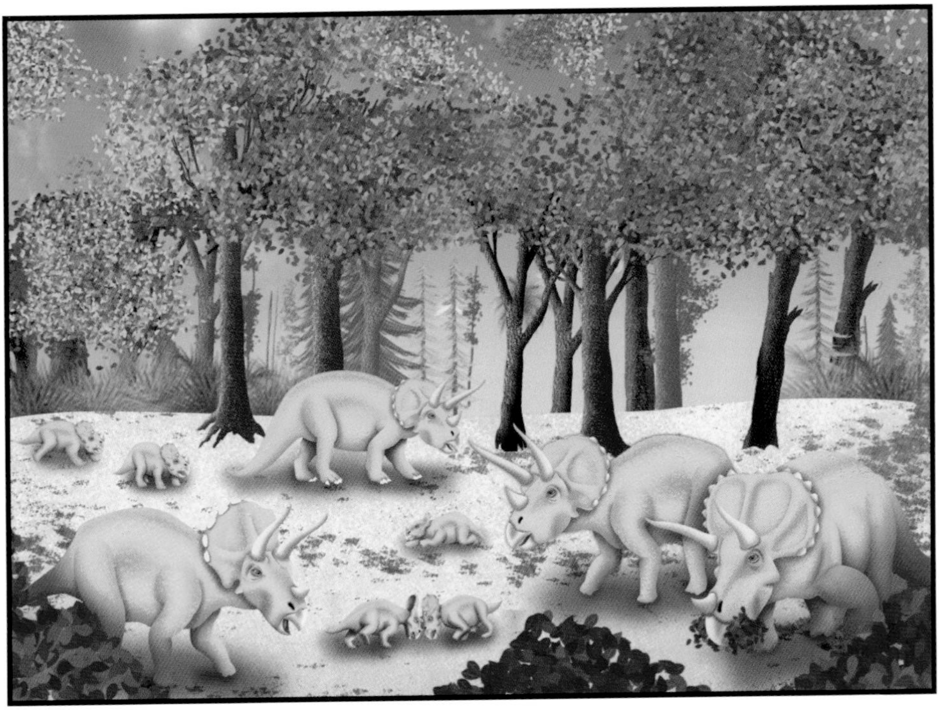

Living in herds helped keep triceratops safe.

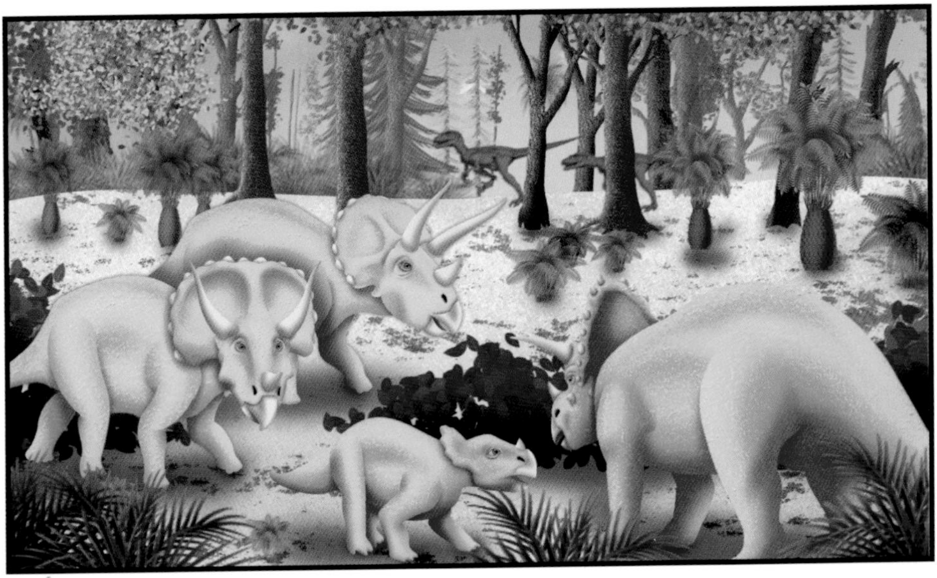

Few dinosaurs dared to attack a triceratops.

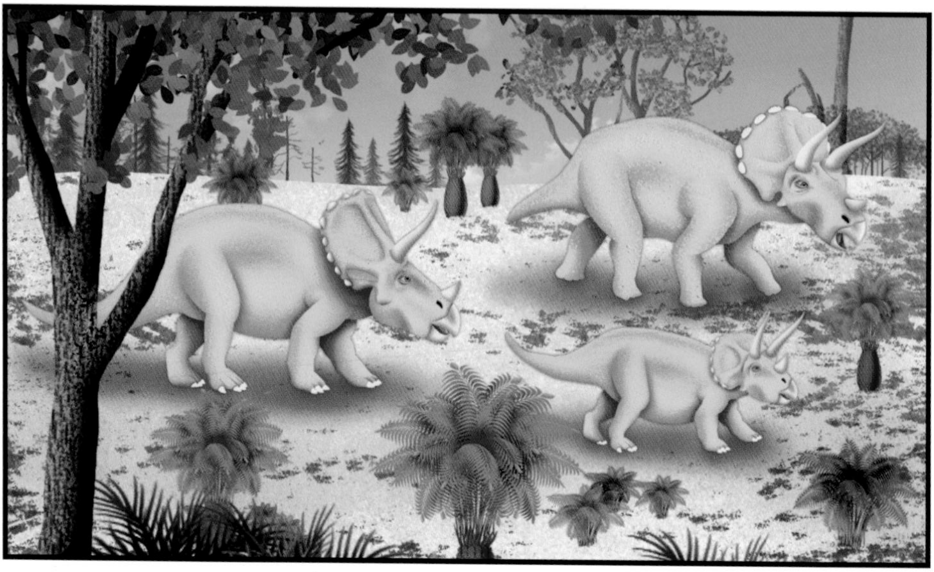

But one dinosaur waited for a chance to grab a big meal.

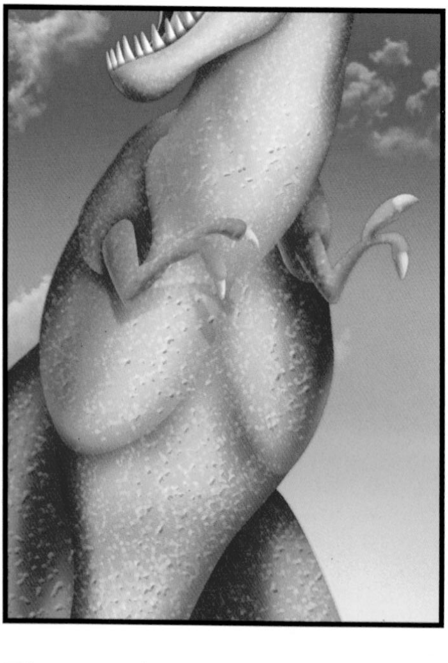

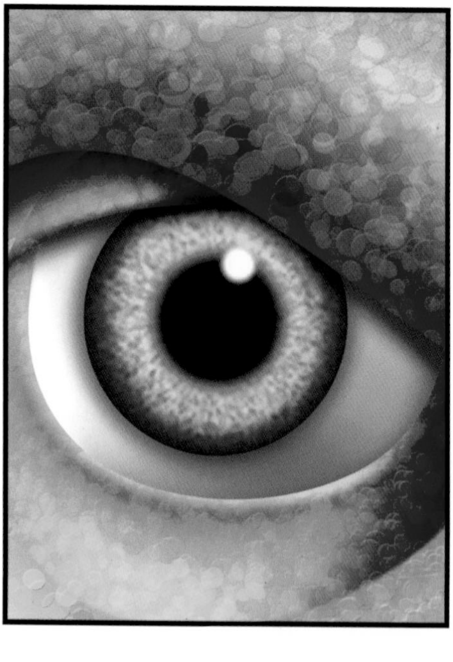

The predator watched for a young or weak triceratops.

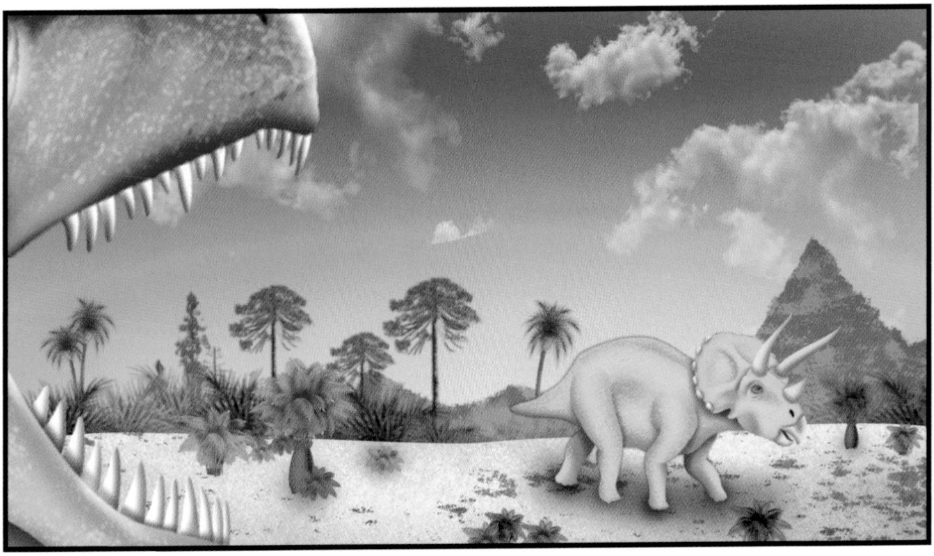

Tyrannosaurus rex was triceratops' number one enemy. And T. rex was always hungry!

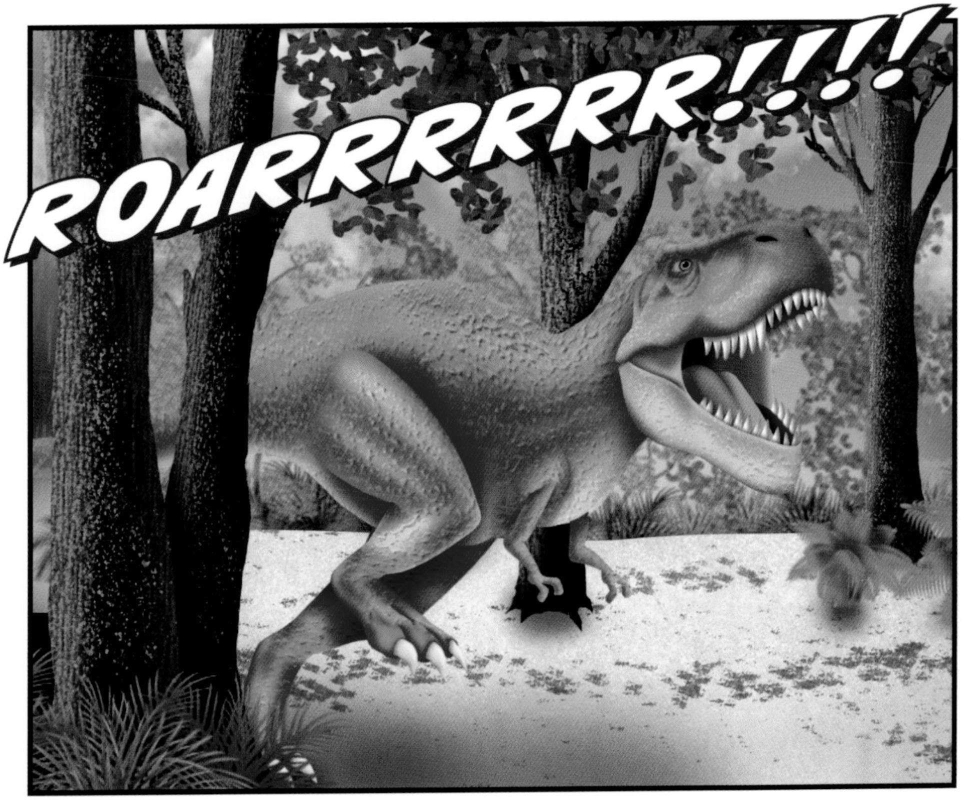
ROARRRRRRR!!!!

The triceratops formed a circle to protect their young.

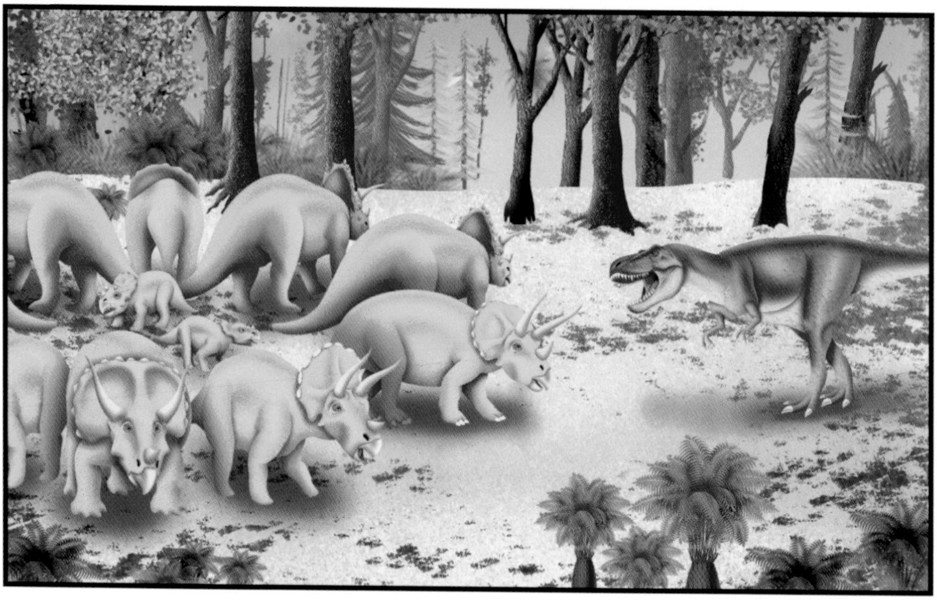

They pointed their sharp horns at T. rex.

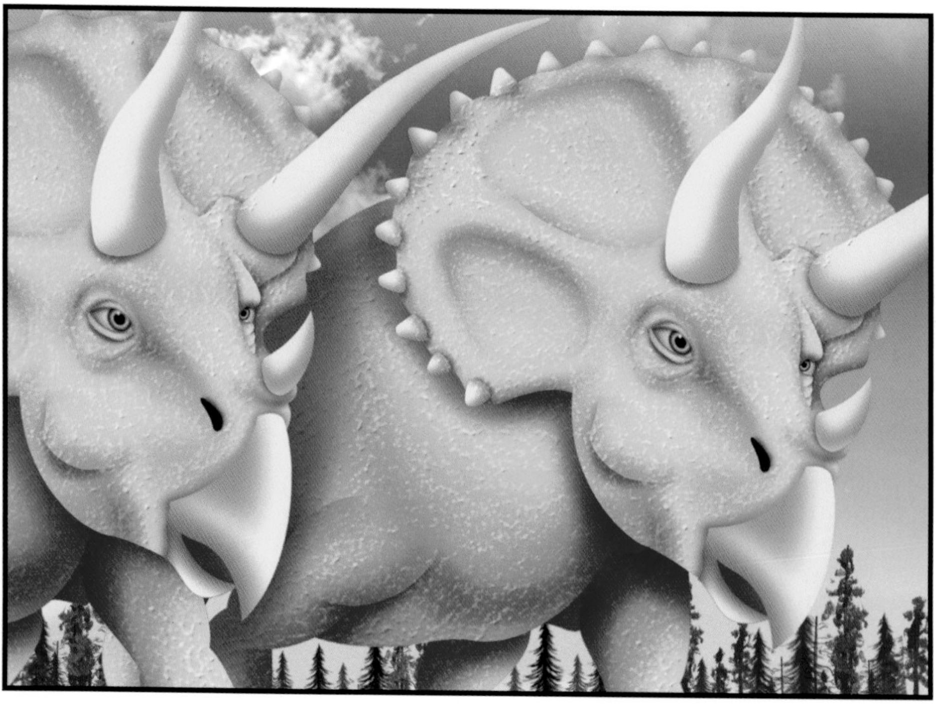

A layer of keratin doubled the length of triceratops' horns. The horns were 3 feet (0.9 m) long.

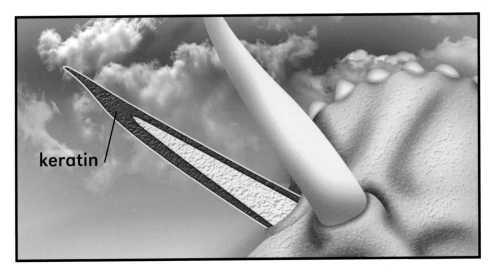

keratin

T. rex's teeth were 9 inches (23 centimeters) long. Were they a match for triceratops' horns?

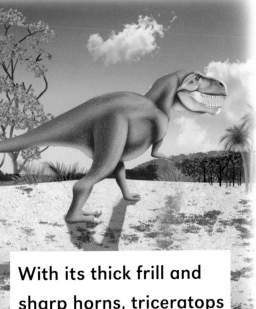

With its thick frill and sharp horns, triceratops was a tough dinosaur!

WHERE IS TRICERATOPS NOW?

Today triceratops are seen only in museums. All the giant dinosaurs died about 65 million years ago.

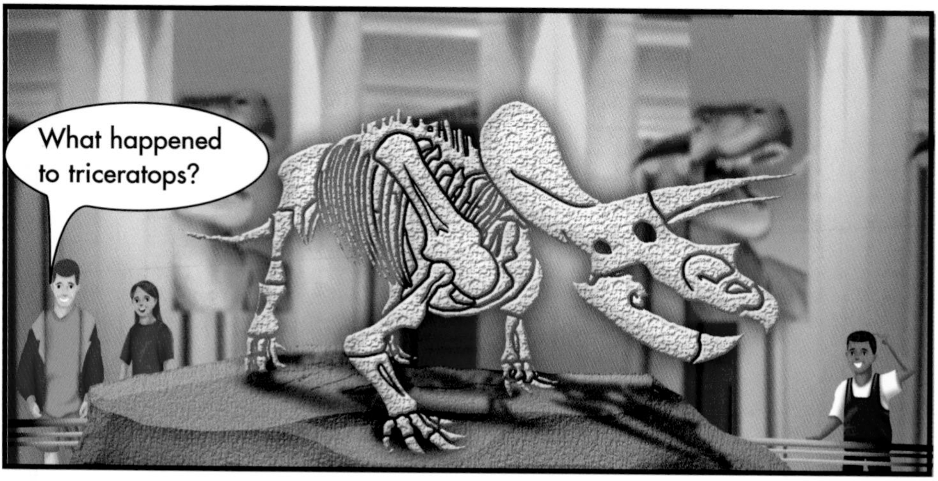
What happened to triceratops?

Scientists think a huge meteorite may have killed the dinosaurs.

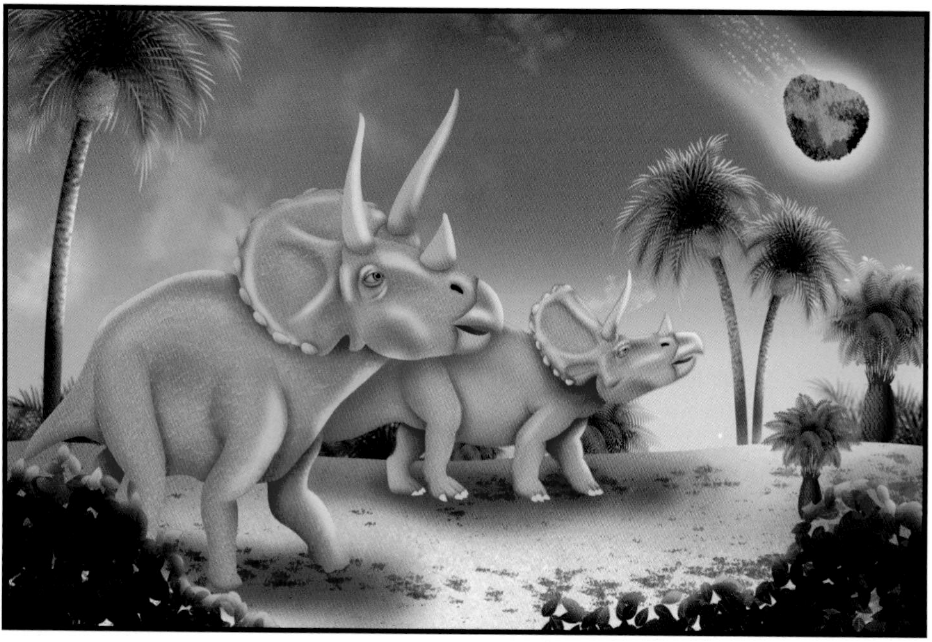

When the meteorite hit Earth, it caused a huge wildfire.

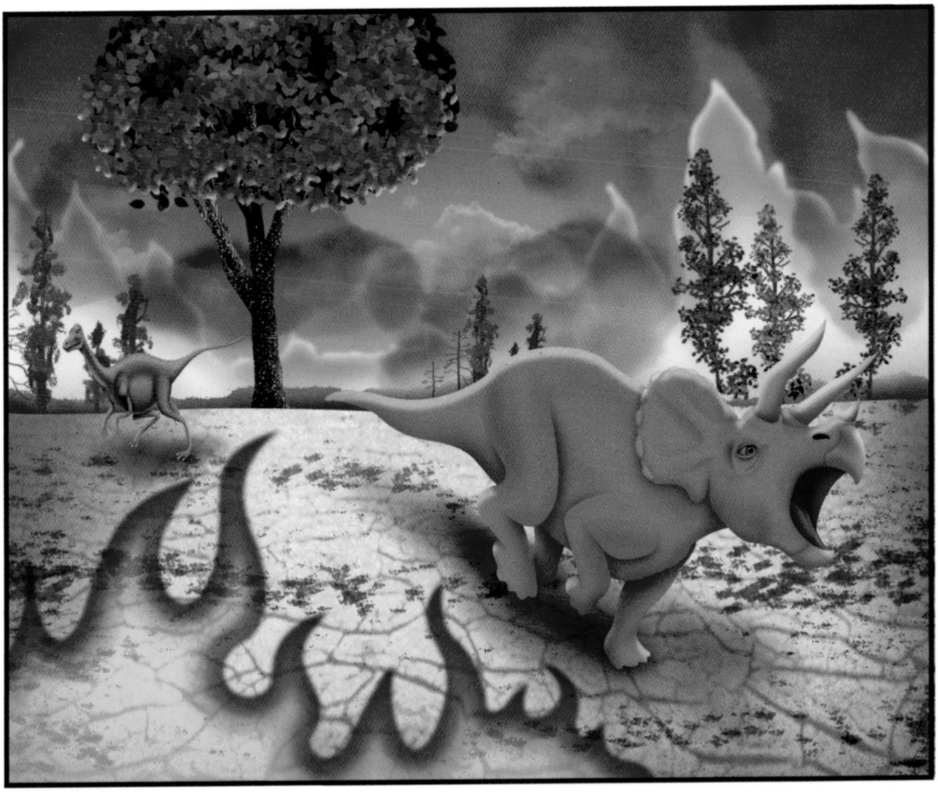

Watering holes dried up. Food was hard to find.

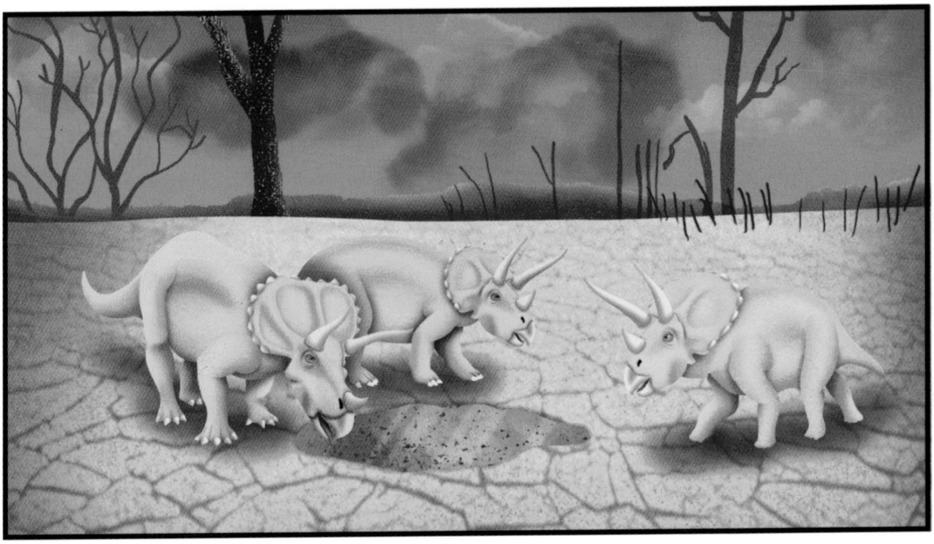

Ash from the meteorite hid the sun. Earth quickly got cold. Plants that didn't burn soon died.

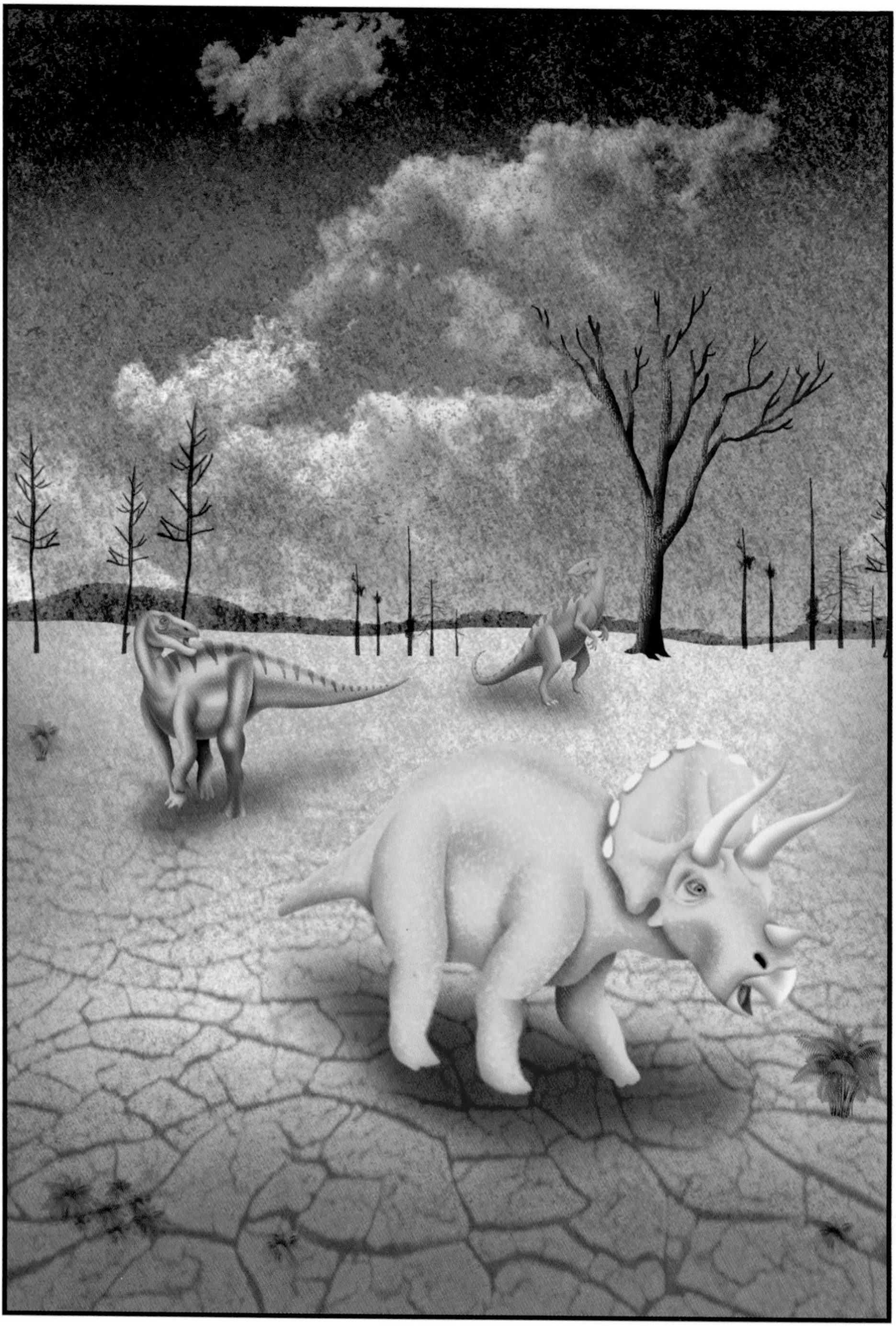

Seventy-five percent of all life on Earth died.
The dinosaurs disappeared.

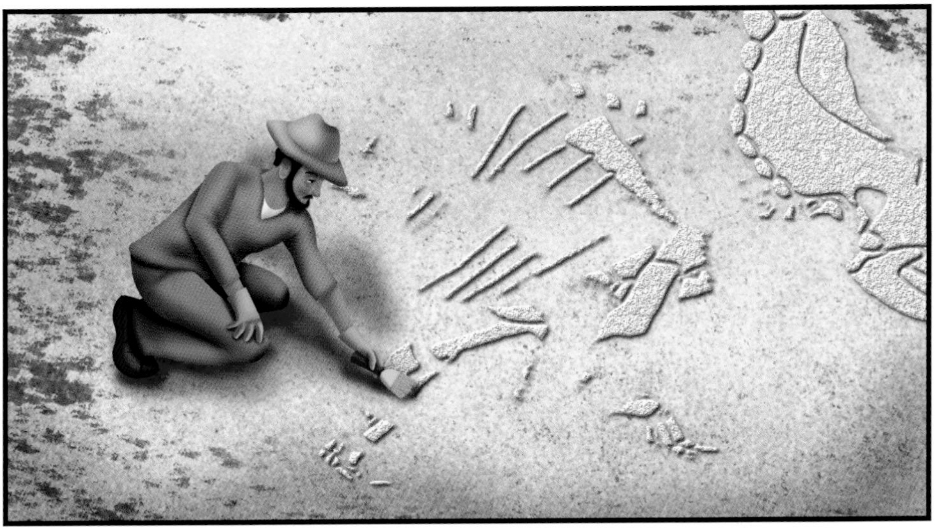

People may never know everything about triceratops.
But scientists continue to learn more about these three-horned giants.

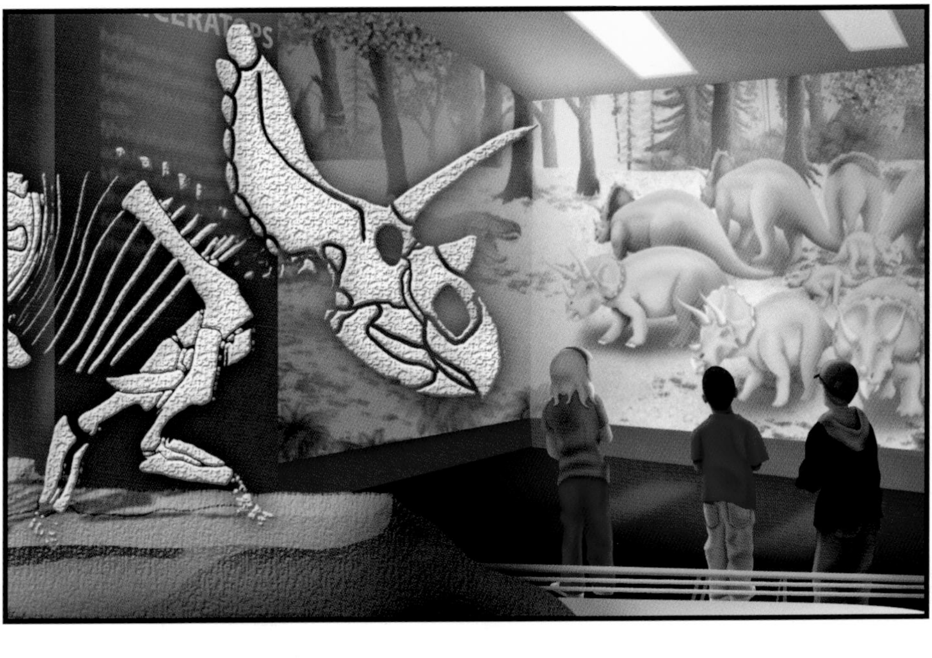

GLOSSARY

ash—a powder that results from an explosion; ash comes out of a volcano when it erupts

beak—the hard front part of the mouth of birds and some dinosaurs

frill—a bony collar that fans out around an animal's neck

hatch—to break out of an egg

herd—a large group of animals that lives or moves together

keratin—the hard substance that forms hair and fingernails in humans

meteorite—a chunk of rock from space that hits a planet

predator—an animal that hunts other animals for food

READ MORE

Dodson, Peter. *Triceratops Up Close: Horned Dinosaur.* Zoom in on Dinosaurs! Berkeley Heights, N.J.: Enslow Publishers, 2011.

Lee, Sally. *The Pebble First Guide to Dinosaurs.* First Guides. Mankato, Minn.: Capstone Press, 2010.

Rockwood, Leigh. *Triceratops.* Dinosaurs Ruled! New York: PowerKids Press, 2012.

INTERNET SITES

FactHound offers a safe, fun way to find Internet sites related to this book. All of the sites on FactHound have been researched by our staff.

Here's all you do:

Visit *www.facthound.com*

Type in this code: 9781429676014

Check out projects, games and lots more at
www.capstonekids.com

INDEX

TITLES IN THIS SET:

Stegosaurus:
Armored Defender

Tyrannosaurus Rex:
Mighty Meat-Eater

Triceratops:
Three-Horned Giant

Velociraptor:
Clawed Hunter

FIRST GRAPHICS

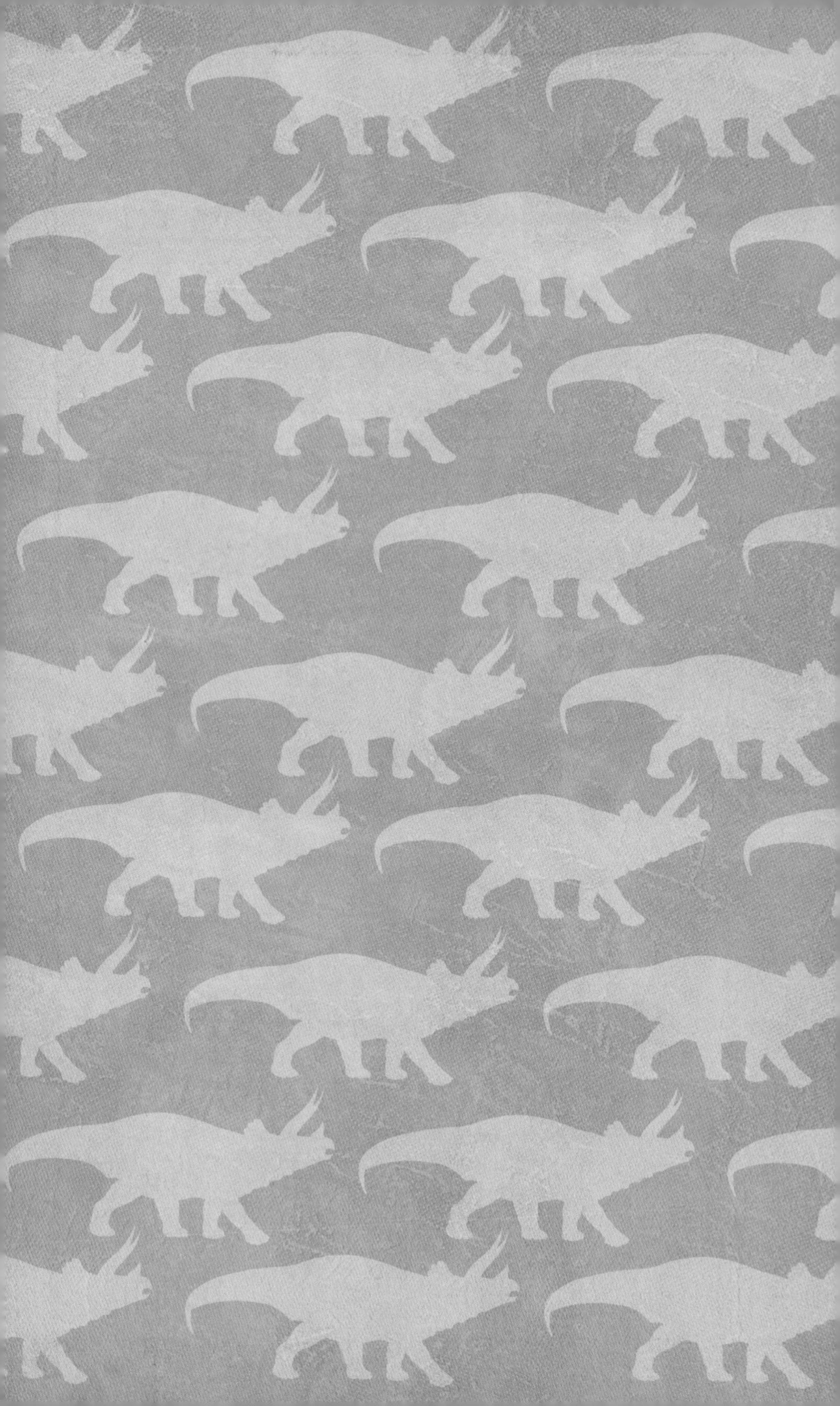